for gabriel

exordium

we are librarians
each time we reshelve a book
a new library card
slipped into well-worn pages
on each card
a new library
at each library
a new collection of cards
infinity wound

before everything is everything

i have a memory
or it is we
or are they all
us

you dont know its the apocalypse when its happening

memory

i dont remember exactly but my brother fell up the stairs while calling for help and he was dead at the hospital four hours later and no one knew why

i wasnt there to hear him land

ever

she has brown skin and icicle eyes and she holds time in her hands
like stones unthrown
mantra of beating drums
and
mountain moving heartbeat
and
fallen friends masked by marching
she is what humanity will look in mirrors to see
she is danger to porcelain pioneers
fingers interlocked with amber allies
moving
unstoppable
to destiny
from darkness

he wraps wounds with his love and dries away the tears
brittle bone magician
healer of trauma
and
shielder of faith
and
bringer of hope
he is the soul that unties black and brown bodies
he is stone heart for reconciliation
strength in stoicism
still
unmoving
to destiny
from darkness

they have bullets in their words and they dream the heart poetic
defining nasturtium now
breath of pioneer
and
wise wordsmith
and
maker of marks
they are the nightmare of status quo
they are the writers of destiny
kintsugi
warrior

to destiny
from darkness

in the future, ever

memory

i dont remember exactly but when you watch a grief counselor tell your dad that his favorite son is dead it makes him human and fragile and you understand for the first time everything he has been hiding

you dont let yourself cry until later because you are a fixer and the only thing you can do right now is be strong for everyone else

cimarron

before: the wild.
rolling hills and big sky
when it rained it must have been a sight to behold
curtains as far as the eye could see
i wonder how people traversed here
rocky mountains and mesas
no sign of what comes next
if anything
a desolation of opportunity
where would they be going?
where would they be coming from?

now: loneliness.
driving on highway 50 in the dark of night
only podcasts and electric vehicles
trails of shuttles clouding cloudless night
moving forward
slowly
wondering what would happen if I just let go
drive off the side
and into the past
some of it must be untouched still
peaceful patches of ignorance.

then: memory.
bodies buried
were they always here?
scarred land
those people died here
they tried to escape but they did not make it
they tried to hide from inevitability
the peace is intact
but there is horror underneath
i can hear the screams.
They are deafening.

memory

i dont remember exactly but when i think of him my eyes fill with the sound of a
song from a video game that i swore i would never forget

i hope that he looks down and is proud of me but im afraid that he is not

elephant bones

heaving
and
breathless
rounded stomach rising and falling
circle of peers
watching

death

they mourn
watching light fade
discordant trumpeting
stomping

Oh little ones, run
while you still can
while the memory is in your brain
and not in the bones

in   twenty years you will come back here
and you will show your young

in   forty years you will return
and you will fight for this place

in   sixty years they will guide you
and you will not see it with your eyes

you will feel it

memory

i dont remember exactly but when i walked to school there was a purple bush with small teardrop leaves that i would snack on because they were sour and bitter and it was like i discovered something new

my brother would not try them with me because he said they were poisonous

found

they
touched
me
but not the way you think.
I was the favorite.
When they first came and no one knew except the government
I listened
I found them in the alley behind my house
and they took me.
I liked the metal instruments.
I liked how they made me feel.

when we went to war
I fought for them.
My friends said I was wrong
but I was not.
I got kicked out
but I was happy to live on the street
against the government
for them
because they always came back
they always checked in.

when they said it was all fake
I did not believe them
Because the government lies
and they still talk to me
they make me feel like everything is okay

it doesn't matter what they think.

memory

i dont remember exactly but my mom let us pick out one thing to buy at the dollar store because we walked all the way there with her and carried the groceries home and i chose black cassette tapes

i would tell stories to myself in the closet and record them because it made me feel like i had a purpose

words written on a steamed living room window to my neighbor in the snow

hi.   /
                                              hey.

no school.   \
                                               :)

snowball fight?   /
                                            cant

why not?   \
                                     mom said no.

:(/
                                          i know.

snowman   \
                                            cant

come over   /
                                            cant

shovel snow   \
                                            cant

this sucks.   /
                                             ya

no school   \
                                          i know

never happens.   /
                                          i know.

gray snow   \
                                          i know

never happens   /
                                          i know

i might play outside   \
                                     mom says no

why?   /
                                      not snow

what?   \
                                mom says not snow

but its cold   /
                                       i know

so snow.   \
                                 it doesnt snow here

until now   /
                                mom says not snow

memory

i dont remember exactly but the silence of hearing my heart break is the loudest sound of all.

Present Darkness Aside

If she is a butterfly then she is my butterfly.

                    Broken winged goddess
          tempting fate.

When she stands
but a glimmer on a pedestal
I am rapt.

If she is a storm then she is my storm.

                    Destruction personified:
          cataclysmic.

She breaks down walls
with a flick of her wrist.
I obey.

If she is the future then she is my future.

memory

i dont remember exactly but i went to sleep on the top bunk and dreamt i was falling from the sky and no one was interested in saving me

i woke up on the floor

the moment she understood the future

"mommy"
        she asked
:are they going to be okay?

:yes
        i said
"if they weren't white they would be dead."

and then we watched and i counted the moments where i would have been dead


```
        1 2      3  4  5      6 7 8 9 10 11 12 13    14 15 16   17  18 19
20            21  22  23  24    25  2627    28  29   303132 33    34
35     36   373839    40    41    42  43  4445    46    4748    4950  51
525354  55  5657        58  5960  6162  63  646566  6768  6970    71
72 73   74 75    76   777879808182838485868788899091 92   93  9495
969798  99 100 101 102 103 104105 106 107 108 109    110    111  112
113114 115  116  117  118119 120 121    122123124125126 127 128
129130131          132 133 134 135  136          137    138139
140 142 142  143   144145  146147  148 149 150 151      152  153   154
155 156  157158159160 161    162  163 164   165  166 167168169   170
171  172   173 174175176   177   178 179  180    181182 183 184  185
186  187  188  189 190 191 192  193 194  195196197        198   199
200  201 202203204205206207  208 209 210 211 212 213214  215  216217
218219220 221  222  223   224
225    226      227                228    229        230
230  231      232                  233              234
235              236                237    238
239          240   241                242
243                244       245
246                      247    248    249
250      251            252              253
```

memory

i dont remember exactly but when my dad drank antifreeze outside of her house
while the police watched i knew that everything wasnt going to be okay even though
i liked her

she couldnt fix us

how many couches see the beginnings of villains

in cushions and wooden frames

guns underneath and over and inside and between
    thoughts of destruction in silent minds as they sit
        loneliness personified
            developing a taste for killing in bottles of alcohol
                drops of blood soaked into cheap foam
                        television reminders that life is not always worth living
                            upturned and taking blows
                                    hands gripped too tightly against corners
                                        naked flesh moving up and then down
                                            chasms filled to the brim
                                                dangerous liaisons
                                                  tipped toes
                                                    heavy
                                                     breathing
                                                     machine gun
                                                    heartbeats

memory

i dont remember exactly but there is discomfort in the space between laughs

do you believe in god?

my god isnt all seeing or all hearing or all knowing
my god is not benevolence or malevolence
my god does not look upon some as worthy and some as not
or make eternal proclamations based on who likes them best
in the shadow of the end of civilization
or in the back alleys of churches
as if there is a difference

  my god is a glint in the eye of a child and the smell of the earth after rain
  my god is baikal stones and the infinite unknown underneath
  my god is whispers from the one you love but who does not yet love you back
  my god is summer storms with best friends in the middle of a park soaking wet
  my god is the qiantang river and natural geometric convalescence
  my god is photos triggering memories triggering tears triggering phone calls
    my god is a solitary moment of peace in a mind fraught with war
    my god is returning home
    my god is
    my god is
    my god is
    my god is
    my god is
    my god is
    my god is
    my god is
    my god is
    my god is
    my god is
    my god is
    my god is
    my god is
    my god is
    my god is
    my god is
    my god is
    my god is
    my god is

yes

memory

i dont remember exactly but my dad held me down while my little brother kicked
me in the face because him and i were fighting and i was winning

my nose bled

no word

wen lang is all loss an tere is no place to fine
wen no one walk an we membr onlee wat we do
not wat we tink
if time is loss too
an life jus storm to storm
an no have gud leadr
an fite
an no one to eat sin
an grup die

I blow love to u wit no word

memory

i dont remember exactly but we would run around and pretend to be ninjas or wrestlers or super saiyan on the weekends as long as we went to check in when the sun was setting

i have a dragonfly on my back to remember the wings you gave me when i was not as strong

where were the heroes in their capes and righteousness when it was all falling down

like

todaler

toy

blocks